HORSE RACING DIARY UK 2022

Calendar, Planner and an Annual
Betting Logbook for all the Horse
Race Betting Enthusiast

THIS DIARY BELONGS TO:

MONTH	MAJOR HORSE RACING EVENTS IN 2022
MARCH	Cheltenham Festival 15. – 18. March
APRIL	Grand National - 9. April All-Weather Champs Finals Day - 15. April
MAY	The Guineas Festival - 30. April – 1. May Dante Festival - 11. – 13. May
JUNE	Epsom Derby Festival - 3. June – 4. June Royal Ascot - 14. June – 18. June
JULY	Glorious Goodwood 26. July – 30. July
AUGUST	Ebor Festival 17. – 20. August
SEPTEMBER	St Leger Festival 7. – 10. September
OCTOBER	British Champions Day 15th October 2022
NOVEMBER	The Open Meeting - Mid-November Betfair Chase - Late November
DECEMBER	King George VI Chase - 26. December Welsh Grand National - Late December

JANUARY

S	M	T	W	T	F	S
						1
2	3	4	5	6	7	8
9	10	11	12	13	14	15
16	17	18	19	20	21	22
23	24	25	26	27	28	29
30	31					

FEBRUARY

S	M	T	W	T	F	S
		1	2	3	4	5
6	7	8	9	10	11	12
13	14	15	16	17	18	19
20	21	22	23	24	25	26
27	28					

APRIL

S	M	T	W	T	F	S
					1	2
3	4	5	6	7	8	9
10	11	12	13	14	15	16
17	18	19	20	21	22	23
24	25	26	27	28	29	30

MARCH

S	M	T	W	T	F	S
		1	2	3	4	5
6	7	8	9	10	11	12
13	14	15	16	17	18	19
20	21	22	23	24	25	26
27	28	29	30	31		

MAY

S	M	T	W	T	F	S
1	2	3	4	5	6	7
8	9	10	11	12	13	14
15	16	17	18	19	20	21
22	23	24	25	26	27	28
29	30	31				

JUNE

S	M	T	W	T	F	S
			1	2	3	4
5	6	7	8	9	10	11
12	13	14	15	16	17	18
19	20	21	22	23	24	25
26	27	28	29	30		

JULY

S	M	T	W	T	F	S
					1	2
3	4	5	6	7	8	9
10	11	12	13	14	15	16
17	18	19	20	21	22	23
24	25	26	27	28	29	30
31						

AUGUST

S	M	T	W	T	F	S
	1	2	3	4	5	6
7	8	9	10	11	12	13
14	15	16	17	18	19	20
21	22	23	24	25	26	27
28	29	30	31			

SEPTEMBER

S	M	T	W	T	F	S
				1	2	3
4	5	6	7	8	9	10
11	12	13	14	15	16	17
18	19	20	21	22	23	24
25	26	27	28	29	30	

OCTOBER

S	M	T	W	T	F	S
						1
2	3	4	5	6	7	8
9	10	11	12	13	14	15
16	17	18	19	20	21	22
23	24	25	26	27	28	29
30	31					

NOVEMBER

S	M	T	W	T	F	S
		1	2	3	4	5
6	7	8	9	10	11	12
13	14	15	16	17	18	19
20	21	22	23	24	25	26
27	28	29	30			

DECEMBER

S	M	T	W	T	F	S
				1	2	3
4	5	6	7	8	9	10
11	12	13	14	15	16	17
18	19	20	21	22	23	24
25	26	27	28	29	30	31

PROFIT/LOSS TRACKER

JANUARY	
FEBRUARY	
MARCH	
APRIL	
MAY	
JUNE	
JULY	
AUGUST	
SEPTEMBER	
OCTOBER	
NOVEMBER	
DECEMBER	

WEBSITES & PASSWORDS

WEBSITE	USERNAME	PASSWORD

WEBSITE	USERNAME	PASSWORD

WEBSITE	USERNAME	PASSWORD

EARNINGS

DATE	BOOK-MAKER	HORSE	ODDS	STAKE	RESULT

DATE	BOOK-MAKER	HORSE	ODDS	STAKE	RESULT

DATE	BOOK-MAKER	HORSE	ODDS	STAKE	RESULT

DATE	BOOK-MAKER	HORSE	ODDS	STAKE	RESULT

DATE	BOOK-MAKER	HORSE	ODDS	STAKE	RESULT

DATE	BOOK-MAKER	HORSE	ODDS	STAKE	RESULT

DATE	BOOK-MAKER	HORSE	ODDS	STAKE	RESULT

DATE	BOOK-MAKER	HORSE	ODDS	STAKE	RESULT

DATE	BOOK-MAKER	HORSE	ODDS	STAKE	RESULT

DATE	BOOK-MAKER	HORSE	ODDS	STAKE	RESULT

MY HORSES

NAME	BREED	BIRTHDAY

NAME	BREED	BIRTHDAY

NAME	BREED	BIRTHDAY

NAME	BREED	BIRTHDAY

NAME	BREED	BIRTHDAY

ODDS CONVERTER CHART

1/10	1.10	1/1	2.00	5/1	6.00
1/9	1.11	11/10	2.10	11/2	6.50
1/8	1.12	6/5	2.20	6/1	7.00
1/7	1.14	5/4	2.25	13/2	7.50
1/6	1.17	11/8	2.38	7/1	8.00
1/5	1.20	6/4	2.50	15/2	8.50
2/9	1.22	13/8	2.63	8/1	9.00
1/4	1.25	7/4	2.75	17/2	9.50
2/7	1.29	9/5	2.80	9/1	10.00
3/10	1.30	15/8	2.86	10/1	11.00
1/3	1.33	2/1	3.00	11/1	12.00
4/11	1.36	85/40	3.12	12/1	13.00
2/5	1.40	11/5	3.20	14/1	15.00
4/9	1.44	9/4	3.25	15/1	16.00
1/2	1.50	12/5	3.40	16/1	17.00
8/15	1.53	5/2	3.50	18/1	19.00
4/7	1.57	13/5	3.60	20/1	21.00
8/13	1.62	11/4	3.75	25/1	26.00
4/6	1.67	3/1	4.00	33/1	34.00
8/11	1.73	10/3	4.33	40/1	41.00
4/5	1.80	7/2	4.50	50/1	51.00
5/6	1.83	4/1	5.00	66/1	67.00
10/11	1.91	9/2	5.50	100/1	101.00

NOTES

BEST HORSE RACING BETTING SITES

These are the best horse racing betting sites in the UK right now:

1. **888Sport** – First past the post

2. **Kwiff** – 2nd Place Refund promotion

3. **Betfred** – The Bonus King of horse racing

4. **Tote** – Pool betting horse racing bonus

5. **Boylesports** – Horse racing offers galore

6. **QuinnBet** – Live stream horse racing for free

7. **William Hill** – Plenty of horse racing promotions

8. **Virgin Bet** – 3/1 winner bonus every day

9. **Spreadex** – Back horses to win by distances

10. **BetUK** – Each Way Plus promo

Printed in Great Britain
by Amazon